Cada Niño
Every Child

A BILINGUAL SONGBOOK
FOR KIDS

Cada Niño
Every Child

A BILINGUAL SONGBOOK
FOR KIDS
BY

TISH HINOJOSA

ILLUSTRATED BY
LUCIA ANGELA PEREZ

*For contact and discography information,
visit Tish Hinojosa's web site:* **www.mundotish.com**

*All of the songs contained in this book have been recorded and are available on
Cada Niño / Every Child, a Rounder Kids CD 8032.* **www.rounder.com**

NATIONAL
ENDOWMENT
FOR THE
ARTS
*This book is funded in part
by generous support from the
National Endowment for the Arts*

For more information, visit our website at
www.cincopuntos.com
or call 1-800-566-9072.

*Cover and book design by Vicki Trego Hill of El Paso, Texas.
Music transcribed by Ricardo Valencia, MusE: Music Editions; musiceditions@aol.com.
Thanks for all your steady work, Ricardo. Many people contributed to make this book a
possibility, among them Rose Hill, Joe Hayes, Ann Morrison, and Gloria Osuna Perez
(whose inspiration continues). Thanks to Eida de la Vega and Antonio Garza for
their careful editing. Printed in Hong Kong by Morris Printing.*

ISBN 0-938317-79-2 • FIRST EDITION • 10 9 8 7 6 5 4 3 2 1

Words and music for "Nina Violina," "Magnolia," "Simplemente Por Amor / Simply for Love," "Hasta Los Muertos Salen A Baila / Even the Dead are
Rising Up to Dance," "¿Quien? / Who?," "Las Fronterizas / The Frontier Women," and "Siempre Abuelita / Always Grandma" by Tish Hinojosa,
© 1996 WB Music Corp. and Manazo Music. Music for "Cada Niño / Every Child," written by Robert Skiles; words by Tish Hinojosa, © 1996 WB Music
Corp. and Manazo Music. "Escala Musical," public domain, adaptation, English translation and arrangement by Tish Hinojosa; "Señora Santa Ana,"
public domain, English translation by Tish Hinojosa, © 1996 WB Music Corp. and Manazo Music. All rights on the preceding songs on behalf of
Manazo Music, administered by WB Music Corp. All rights reserved. Used by permission Warner Bros. Publications U.S. Inc., Miami, Florida 33014.
Words and music for "Barnyard Dance / El Baile Vegetal" by Carl Martín, © 1980 by Flying Fish. All rights reserved. Used by permission
Happy Valley Music, Ltd; Cambridge, MA 02140. Spanish translation by Tish Hinojosa with permission.

A Note from Tish

WHEN I WAS SEVEN, I wanted to be a scientist or an astronomer. Secretly though, I would go way out in the backyard near the San Antonio River and sing songs I learned from my favorite movies. These songs and movies were in English and in Spanish.

My parents came to America from Mexico, and I was born and raised in San Antonio, so it was very natural for me to feel a sense of belonging to both the Mexican and the American cultures. But I admit that there were times when I found myself feeling uncomfortable or different around some kids or grown-ups, because part of me was connected to a world different from theirs. As time went by, I learned that this difference helped me understand other people, who for many reasons have their own special stories. I grew confident and took pride in who I was.

By the time I was a teenager, I was playing guitar and singing for people. A little later, I began writing my own songs. I've had a chance to sing these songs in many cities across the United States, and in some far-away countries. Maybe someday I'll study more science or astronomy. Right now I'm enjoying making music and my other job: being a mom. I hope you like these songs.

A LOS SIETE AÑOS quería ser científica o astrónoma. Pero, en secreto, pasaba el tiempo en el solar de mi casa cerca del río San Antonio cantando las canciones que había aprendido de mis películas favoritas. Esas canciones las cantaba en inglés y en español.

Mis padres habían venido a los Estados Unidos desde México. Yo había nacido y crecido en San Antonio, Texas, por lo que, para mí, era muy natural sentirme parte de las dos culturas: la norteamericana y la mexicana. Pero a veces, cuando estaba con ciertos niños o adultos, me sentía extraña, diferente, porque una parte de mí pertenecía a un mundo muy distinto al de ellos. Con el tiempo, entendí que esta diferencia me ayudaba a comprender a otras personas con historias tan especiales como la mía. Entonces, crecí con la confianza y el orgullo de ser quien soy.

A los dieciséis años ya estaba tocando la guitarra y cantando en público. Un poco después, empecé a componer mis propias canciones. He tenido la suerte de cantar estas canciones en ciudades de todo el país y también en países lejanos. Quizás algún día estudie ciencia o astronomía. Por ahora me divierto creando música y también me dedico a mi otro trabajo: el de ser mamá. Espero que te gusten estas canciones.

To my children—"pedazos de mi corazón."
Thank you for making parenting such an adventure.
—TISH HINOJOSA

~

To all who have given me strength.
—LUCIA ANGELA PEREZ

Contents

Cada Niño  Every Child

Music by Robert Skiles
Lyrics by Tish Hinojosa

MY FRIEND and music composer, Robert "Beto" Skiles, wrote this song as an instrumental for his daughter, Lucy. It was called "Lucy's Song." The first time I heard it, I loved it, and asked him if I could add words, and he said yes. So I took Beto's idea and made it bigger, to be about all kids. P.S. Thank you for sharing your song, Lucy.

MI AMIGO y compositor, Roberto "Beto" Skiles, escribió esta canción como instrumental para su hija, Lucy. Se llamaba "Lucy's Song". Al oírla por primera vez, me encantó, le pregunté si podía agregarle palabras y me dijo que sí. Entonces, tomé la idea de Beto y la extendí para que fuera de todos los niños. P.D. Gracias por compartir tu canción, Lucy.

Ve - o en ca - da ni - ño un por - ve - nir,

es - pe - ran - za fuer - za y paz.

Mi o - cu - pa - ción es dán - do - les ra - zón que la

fe no pier - dan ja - más.

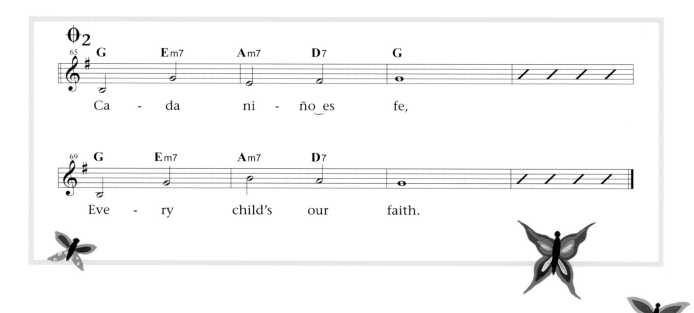

Ca - da ni - ño es fe,

Eve - ry child's our faith.

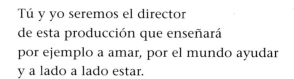

Veo en cada niño un porvenir,
esperanza fuerza y paz.
Mi ocupación es dándoles razón
que la fe no pierdan jamás.

Every child believes in good tomorrow brings,
every child's our faith to hold.
What we leave behind and want for them to find
is what we are today.

Laughter, voices, tender choices,
their love gives to us.
Sad the day we take away
their sweet liberty.

La la la la la la la . . .

Tú y yo seremos el director
de esta producción que enseñará
por ejemplo a amar, por el mundo ayudar
y a lado a lado estar.

Risas, voces, tiernas cosas
que este amor nos da.
Triste el día que quitemos
esa libertad.

Every child believes in good tomorrow brings,
every child's our faith to hold.
What we leave behind and want for them to find
is what we are today.

Cada niño es fe,
every child's our faith.

La la la la la la la . . .

Escala Musical • Music Scale

Traditional

THIS SONG HAS BEEN HEARD on the Texas-Mexico border for a hundred years. The old words written with it talk about romance. I thought it might be fun to change the words to sing about how in Mexico they learn music notes as "do re mi fa sol la si do," and in America we learn C D E F G A B C, but it's the same thing.

ESTA CANCIÓN SE HA ESCUCHADO en la frontera tejano-mexicana por cien años. Las palabras antiguas hablan de romance. Yo pensé que sería divertido cambiar las palabras un poco para enseñar cómo en México se aprenden los tonos de música "do re mi fa sol la si do", y en los Estados Unidos se aprenden C D E F G A B C, pero, en realidad, son la misma cosa.

March ♩ = 120

Vén - gan - se ni - ños, vengan a es - cu - char los
Come, all you chil - dren and hear what I say, in

dul - ces a - cor - des de la es - ca - la mu - si - cal.
har - mo - ny climb - ing up and down the mu - sic scale.

13

Vénganse niños ven a escuchar Los
dulces acordes de la escala
musical

si la sol fa mi re d

do re mi fa sol la si do

Come all you children hear what I say
In harmony climbing up and down
the music scale

Vengan, be - llos ni - ños, muy pron - to me_i - ré.
Come, all you chil - dren, for soon I will go,

Con tu co - ra-zón can - tan-do es - to tú de - bes sa - ber.
let me hear your heart is sing-ing, this is some - thing you should know.

C se can - ta sim-ple - men - te Do, D bai - lan - do de - re -
First the mid-dle C is sim-ply Do, then the D comes danc-ing

chi - ta Re, E es e - le - gan - te así Mi, F flo - re - ci - ta
by Re, E is e - le-gant like this Mi, F ar-rives in flower-y

lle - ga Fa, G ge - ne-ro-sa so - la - na Sol, A mi_a-mor es siem-pre
fash-ion Fa, G is gen-u-ine as sun-shine Sol, A, you'll al-ways have my

tu - yo La, B en es-pa - ñol se di - ce Si, Si La Sol Fa Mi Re
heart La, B in Span-ish it is said Si, Si La Sol Fa Mi Re

Solo

Do.
Do.

15

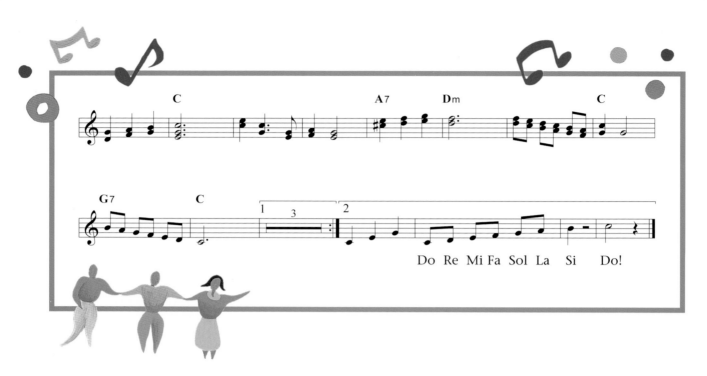

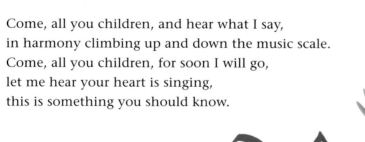

Vénganse niños, vengan a escuchar
los dulces acordes de la escala musical.
Vengan, bellos niños, muy pronto me iré.
Con tu corazón cantando
esto tú debes saber.

C se canta simplemente Do,
D bailando derechita Re,
E es elegante así Mi,
F de florcita llega Fa,
G generosa solana Sol,
A mi amor es siempre tuyo La,
B en español se dice Si,
Si La Sol Fa Mi Re Do.

Come, all you children, and hear what I say,
in harmony climbing up and down the music scale.
Come, all you children, for soon I will go,
let me hear your heart is singing,
this is something you should know.

First the middle C is simply Do,
then the D comes dancing by Re,
E is elegant like this Mi,
F arrives in flowery fashion Fa,
G is genuine as sunshine Sol,
A you'll always have my heart La,
B in Spanish it is said Si,
Si La Sol Fa Mi Re Do.

[End] Do Re Mi Fa Sol La Si Do!

16

Siempre Abuelita
Always Grandma

Music and lyrics by Tish Hinojosa

I HAD THE CHANCE TO KNOW just one of my grandmas, my mother's mother, Dorotea. She lived in a one-room apartment in Nuevo Laredo, Tamaulipas, Mexico. I loved visiting her and sleeping in her steel-framed, cushiony, pillowed bed. She didn't like to cook or clean much, but she liked to drink coffee and tell stories until my eyelids would grow heavy as I sat snugly next to her. My mind—on imagination's wings—would fly out of the open window into the starry quiet night which blanketed the Mexican countryside. I only knew her until I was seven, but I'll always remember her love.

YO CONOCÍ solamente a una de mis abuelas, la mamá de mi mamá, Dorotea. Ella vivía en un apartamentito en Nuevo Laredo, Tamaulipas, México. Me encantaba visitarla y dormir en su cama de hierro llena de almohadas suavecitas. A Dorotea no le gustaba cocinar ni limpiar, pero sí le gustaba mucho tomar café y contarme cuentos hasta que me pesaban los párpados y me quedaba dormida junto a ella. En las alas de la imaginación, mi mente volaba hacia fuera, cruzando el cielo estrellado de la noche que cubría de calma el campo mexicano. Aunque sólo la conocí durante mis primeros siete años, siempre recordaré su amor.

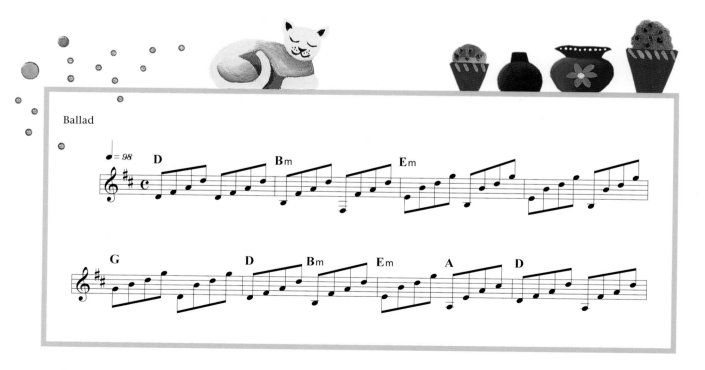

tus son - ri - sas, tus ca - ri - cias, tu mo-do de ser.
full of love, I won't for-get that you have giv - en me.

Lle - na de tu fiel ca - ri - ño no te ol - vi - da - ré.

rit.

Siempre, siempre, abuelita, yo recordaré
tus sonrisas, tus caricias,
tu modo de ser.
Siempre, siempre, abuelita,
por la vida iré,
llena de tu fiel cariño
no te olvidaré.

Always, always, Abuelita, I'll remember true
your embraces, ways, and faces
that belong to you.
Always, always, Abuelita,
all my life I'll be
full of love, I won't forget
that you have given me.

Siempre, siempre, abuelita, yo recordaré
tus sonrisas, tus caricias, tu modo de ser.
Always, always, Abuelita,

all my life I'll be
full of love, I won't forget
that you have given me.
Llena de tu fiel cariño no te olvidaré.

20

El Baile Vegetal
The Barnyard Dance

Music and lyrics by Carl Martin
Spanish translation by Tish Hinojosa

YOU MAY THINK vegetables lead a dull life. But here we find the garden vegetables having a wild party under a late night moon. The most fun part of translating this song to Spanish for me was saying "betabel rojo"—that's "little red beet." You'll never see your salad the same again!

PUEDEN CREER QUE los vegetales viven una vida aburrida. Pero aquí los encontramos en una fiesta a la luz de la luna de medianoche. Lo que más me divirtió fue traducir del inglés al español "little red beet" a "betabel rojo". ¡Desde ahora ya no mirarán a sus ensaladas con los mismos ojos!

It was late one night in the pale moon - light all the
veg - e - tables gave a spree. They put up a sign, said the
dance is at nine and all the ad - mis - sions were free. There were

peas and greens, cab-bage and beans, it was the big-gest crowd you ev-er did see.

When old man cu-cum-ber struck up that num-ber, you

should've heard those veg-e-tables scream! Ahhh! Well, little tur-nip top did the

back-wards flop. The cab-bage shook the shim-my and she could not stop. The little red

beet shook his feet. Wa-ter-mel-on died of the

cock-eyed heat. Little to-ma-ta, a-gi-ta-da,

shook the shim-my with the sweet po-ta-ta. And old man gar-lic dropped

dead of the col - ic   down at the barn - yard   dance,

down   at   the   barn - yard   dance.

1,2,3.

4.

Da Capo al Coda

que fue a - no-che.   Down at the barn-yard   late last night,

el bai - le ve - ge - tal.

24

It was late one night in the pale moonlight
all the vegetables gave a spree.
They put up a sign, said the dance is at nine
and all the admissions were free.
There were peas and greens,
cabbage and beans,
it was the biggest crowd you ever did see.
When old man cucumber
struck up that number,
you should've heard those vegetables scream!

Well, little turnip top did the backwards flop.
The cabbage shook the shimmy
and she could not stop.
The little red beet shook his feet.
Watermelon died of the cock-eyed heat.
Little tomata, agitada,
shook the shimmy with the sweet potata.
And old man garlic dropped dead of the colic
down at the barnyard dance,
down at the barnyard dance.

La cosecha fue al anochecer.
Bajo el claro de la luna bailar.
Dijo el letrero que a las nueve es
y no hay que pagar.
Llegaron chícharo y col,
repollo y frijol: ya muy pronto se perdió el control.
Cuando el gran pepino
dio sonido muy fino
vegetales se oían gritar!

Cebollita vi brincar y maromas dar
la col tembló al ritmo
sin poder parar.
Betabel rojo a sus pies cayó.
Sandía se murió de tanto calor.
Tomatito, chespirito
se dio vuelta con el camotito
y el viejo ajo se perdió en un frasco.
El baile vegetal
que fue anoche.
Down at the barnyard late last night,
el baile vegetal.

FREE
DANCE

Nina Violina

Music and lyrics by Tish Hinojosa

THIS SIMPLE SONG began as a way for my kids to learn and practice Spanish. We would mix music, Spanish and art "class" by writing verses about everyday events (and special occasions) and keeping them in a notebook with pictures to help remember words. My daughter Nina, seven years old, added this song to her Suzuki violin repertoire. Her violin teacher, Amy Tiven, often calls her "Nina Violina."

ESTA CANCIÓN SENCILLA empezó como una manera de hacer que mis niños aprendieran y practicaran el español. Mezclábamos "clases" de música, español y arte. Escribíamos versos sobre cosas de todos los días (y también sobre cosas especiales) y los guardábamos en un cuaderno con dibujos para que ellos luego recordaran las palabras. Mi hija Nina, de siete años, agregó esta pieza a su repertorio de violín Suzuki. Su instructora de violín, Amy Tiven, a veces la llama "Nina Violina".

Nos le-van-ta-mos en la ma-ña-na,
We are a-ris-ing ear-ly this morn-ing,

des-a-yu-na-mos, pan de man-za-na.
ap-ple bread wait-ing, break-fast is call-ing,

Qué bien se sien-te el co-ra-zón,
love in a smile and a heart beating,

por es - te dí - a, por es - te a - mor.
what a good way, each new day be - ginning.

Solo

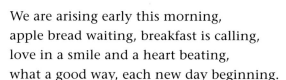

Nos levantamos en la mañana,
desayunamos, pan de manzana.
Qué bien se siente el corazón,
por este día, por este amor.

We are arising early this morning,
apple bread waiting, breakfast is calling,
love in a smile and a heart beating,
what a good way, each new day beginning.

Noche es oscura, oscura es,
pero otro mundo nos deja ver.
Trae las estrellas la luna y el soñar,
y a la madrugada el gallo cantar.

Nighttime is dark, dark is the night,
another world it brings into sight,
starshine and moonshine and dreams it brings,
and when it's dawn, the rooster will sing.

Días y meses las estaciones,
cambian el tiempo, son las razones,
verano, otoño, invierno, primavera
causan los cambios adentro y afuera.

Day and months make up the seasons,
give us the weather, these are the reasons,
summer and fall and winter and spring
cause the changes outside and in.

Ahora es tu turno canta tú aquí,
Nina acompaña en su violín.
Now it's your turn, your turn to sing,
Nina will play it on her violin.

Magnolia

Music and lyrics by Tish Hinojosa

WHEN I WAS GROWING UP, a magnolia tree that grew in our yard shaded a favorite play place for my sister Diana and me. Our daydreams, wishes and secrets rustled and danced through those big shiny leaves and white blossoms on up to the blue borderless sky.

UN ÁRBOL DE MAGNOLIA que crecía en el jardín de la casa de mi niñez daba sombra al lugar donde jugábamos mi hermana Diana y yo. Sueños, deseos y secretos susurraban y bailaban entre las flores blancas y las hojas brillantes hasta alcanzar el cielo azul sin fronteras.

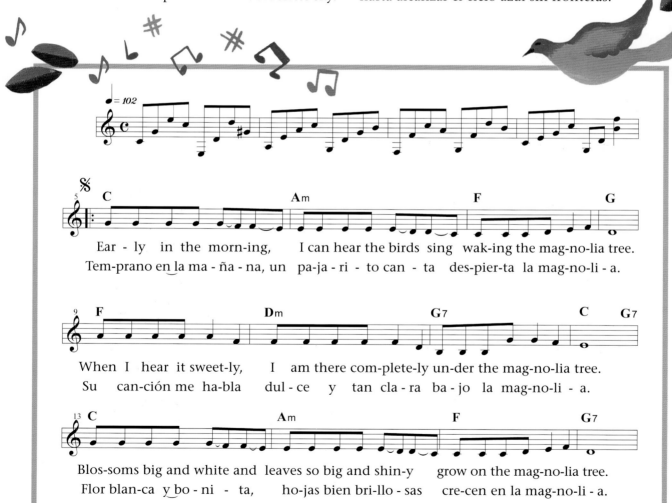

Ear - ly in the morn-ing, I can hear the birds sing wak-ing the mag-no-lia tree.
Tem-prano en la ma - ña - na, un pa-ja - ri - to can - ta des-pier-ta la mag-no-li - a.

When I hear it sweet-ly, I am there com-plete-ly un-der the mag-no-lia tree.
Su can-ción me ha-bla dul - ce y tan cla - ra ba - jo la mag-no-li - a.

Blos-soms big and white and leaves so big and shin-y grow on the mag-no-lia tree.
Flor blan-ca y bo - ni - ta, ho-jas bien bri-llo - sas cre-cen en la mag-no-li - a.

un-der the mag-no - lia   tree.   Fall-ing leaves cre-at-ing   ta-co shells with fill-ing
ba - jo la mag-no-li - a.   Pre-ten - dien-do ho-jas   ta-cos bien sa - bro-sos

un-der the mag-no - lia   tree.   Hmm,   and friends they come to call,
ba - jo la mag-no-li - a.   Hmm,   vie - nen a   vi - si - tar,

hmm,   John, Ring-o, George and Paul. We laugh and watch mag-no-lia dance for
hmm,   John, Ring-o, George y   Paul. Rien - do ve - mos mag-no - li - a bai-

free.   *D.S. al Fine*
lar.

(2nd time) Mag-

no - li - a,   mag - no - li - a,   mag-

no - lia.   Ba - jo la mag-no - lia,   ba - jo la mag-no - lia,

32

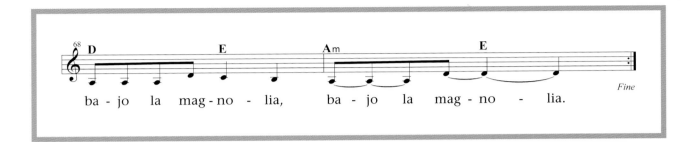

ba - jo   la   mag - no - lia,   ba - jo   la   mag - no - lia.

Fine

Early in the morning, I can hear the birds sing
waking the magnolia tree.
When I hear it sweetly, I am there completely
under the magnolia tree.
Blossoms big and white and leaves so big and shiny
grow on the magnolia tree.
Springtime brings the flowers, I can dream for hours
under the magnolia tree.
Hmm, I see the sky above.
Hmm, and think of what I love.
The wind blows and makes magnolia dance for me.

Summertime is ending, ain't no more pretending
under the magnolia tree.
Autumn leaves are falling, wintertime is calling
under the magnolia tree.
My sister and me, we sit and have some tea here
under the magnolia tree.
Falling leaves creating taco shells with filling
under the magnolia tree
Hmm, and friends they come to call,
hmm, John, Ringo, George, and Paul.
We laugh and watch magnolia dance for free.

Temprano en la mañana, un pajarito canta
despierta la magnolia.
Su canción me habla dulce y tan clara
bajo la magnolia.
Flor blanca y bonita, hojas bien brillosas
crecen en magnolia.

En primavera sola yo sueño durante horas
bajo la magnolia.
Hmm, y miro el cielo allá.
Hmm, y pienso en amar.
El viento baila magnolia para mí.

El verano se acaba, también el juego para
bajo la magnolia.
Hojas caen de otoño, anunciando el invierno
bajo la magnolia.
Mi hermanita y yo con té y desayuno
bajo la magnolia.
Pretendiendo hojas tacos bien sabrosos
bajo la magnolia.
Hmm, vienen a visitar,
hmm, John, Ringo, George y Paul.
Riemos y vemos a magnolia bailar.

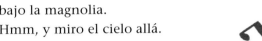

Simplemente por Amor
Simply for Love

Music and lyrics by Tish Hinojosa

THE WONDERFUL THING ABOUT LOVE
is how special it makes us feel.

LA COSA MÁS MARAVILLOSA DEL AMOR
es lo especial que nos hace sentir.

♩ = 94

C   Dm   Em   F

When I tell you   that I love you,   that my heart will   al - ways be
Cuan-do di - go   que te quie - ro,   que mi co - ra - zón   se - rá

C   Dm   Em   G   C

proud-er than I   ev - er dreamed of,   sim-ply with your love   for me.
or - gu - llo - so   sim - ple - men - te   por a - mor   que tu   me das.

34

Cuan-do llue - ve, when the rain falls, bri-llas co - mo el sol.

It's your smil - e, tu son - ri - sa shin-ing like the sun.

When I tell you that I love you, that my heart will al - ways be

proud-er than I ev - er dreamed of, sim-ply with your love for me.

Or-gu - llo - so sim - ple - men - te por a - mor que tu me das.

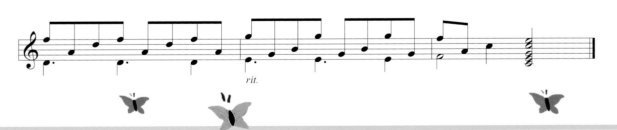

rit.

When I tell you that I love you,
that my heart will always be
prouder than I ever dreamed of,
simply with your love for me.

Cuando digo que te quiero,
que mi corazón estará
orgulloso simplemente
por el amor que tú me das.

Cuando llueve,
when the rain falls,
brillas como el sol.
It's your smile,
tu sonrisa
shining like the sun.

Cuando digo que te quiero,
que mi corazón estará
orgulloso simplemente
por el amor que tú me das.

Cuando llueve,
when the rain falls,
brillas como el sol.
It's your smile,
tu sonrisa
shining like the sun.

When I tell you that I love you,
that my heart will always be
prouder than I ever dreamed of,
simply with your love for me.
Orgulloso simplemente
por el amor que tú me das.

Hasta Los Muertos Salen a Bailar
Even the Dead are Rising Up to Dance

Music and lyrics by Tish Hinojosa

"THE DAY OF THE DEAD" takes place the day after Halloween. It is celebrated in many Latin American countries by visiting ancestors in graveyards and bringing flowers, music, food and decorations.

"EL DÍA DE LOS MUERTOS" se celebra el día después de Halloween. Se festeja en muchos países latinoamericanos con visitas a nuestros antepasados en los camposantos para traerles flores, música, comida y decoraciones.

La lu-na

lle-na a - ca - ba de lle-gar. El o - tro mun-do em-pie - za a des-per-tar. Ba-jo las
san-to, hay que ce-le - brar por-que esta no - che to - do es em-bru-jar. Y el co-

som-bras va - mos a can-tar. Has-ta los muer-tos sa - len a bai-lar. Al cam-po
yo-te em-pie - za a au - llar. Has-ta los muer-tos sa - len a bai - - - - lar.

Flo - res, can - cio - nes, pa - pel de co - lo - res o -
Quie - nes re - cuer - dan a - mo - res, san - tos, pe - ca -

lo - res de an - to - jos que traen.
do - res a - llí va - mos a es - tar.

The moon is full of some-thing on the rise. The oth-er world is o - pen-ing its eyes. Out in the

grave-yard, we will sing a stance. E-ven the dead are ris - ing up to dance.

41

Love songs   and   flow - ers   and   pa - pers, bright col - ors   and
There we   re - mem - ber   the   saints   and   the   sin - ners, this

smells of   the   food that   we   bring.
night   with them we   will sing.

Los em-bru-

ja-dos sa - len a bai - lar.   Y La Llo - ro-na mi - ra don-de está. Ai con la
li-tos sa - len a bai - lar.   Ti - os y ti-as sa - len a bai - lar. Has - ta mon-

mo-mia en - re - da-da va. Has - ta los muer-tos sa - len a bai - lar. Los a-bue-
ji - tas van   de a-llá pa' - ca. Has - ta los muer-tos sa - len a bai - lar. La lu-na

lle-na a - ca - ba de lle - gar.   El o-tro mun-do em-pie-za a des-per-tar. Out in the

grave-yard, we   will sing a stance. E-ven the dead are ris - ing up to dance. Has-ta los

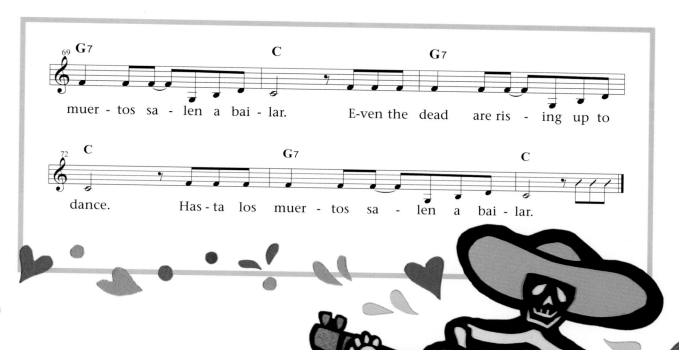

muer - tos sa - len a bai - lar. E-ven the dead are ris - ing up to dance. Has - ta los muer - tos sa - len a bai - lar.

La luna llena acaba de llegar.
El otro mundo empieza a despertar.
Bajo las sombras vamos a cantar.
Hasta los muertos salen a bailar.

Al camposanto, hay que celebrar
porque esta noche todo es embrujar.
Y el coyote empieza a aullar.
Hasta los muertos salen a bailar.

Flores, canciones, papel de colores
olores de antojos que traen.
Quienes recuerdan amores, santos, pecadores
allí vamos a estar.

The moon is full of something on the rise.
The other world is opening its eyes.
Out in the graveyard, we will sing a stance.
Even the dead are rising up to dance.

Love songs and flowers and papers, bright colors
and smells of the food that we bring.
There we remember the saints and the sinners,
this night with them we will sing.

Los embrujados salen a bailar
Y La Llorona mira donde está.
Ahí con la momia enredada va.
Hasta los muertos salen a bailar.

Los abuelitos salen a bailar.
Tíos y tías salen a bailar.
Hasta monjitas van de allá pa'ca.
Hasta los muertos salen a bailar.

La luna llena acaba de llegar.
El otro mundo empieza a despertar.
Out in the graveyard, we will sing a stance.
Even the dead are rising up to dance.

Hasta los muertos salen a bailar.
Even the dead are rising up to dance.
Hasta los muertos salen a bailar.

¿Quién? • Who?

Music and lyrics by Tish Hinojosa

KIDS ASK many good questions. Sometimes grown-ups ask the same ones. It's good to be curious. Even if there aren't always answers.

LOS NIÑOS HACEN muy buenas preguntas. Los adultos, a veces, también. Es bueno tener curiosidad. Aunque no siempre hay respuestas para todo.

♩ = 135

E   F♯   B

B   F♯   B

¿Quién hi - zo tan - tas es - tre - - - llas?
Who made the stars and so man - - - y?

¿Quién le dio o - las al mar?
Who gave the waves to the sea?

¿Quién nos dio ri - sa en el sue - - ño?
Who makes us laugh when we're dream - - - ing?

¿Quién nos dio tan - to que pen - sar?
Who makes us think of these things?

Hum - - - - - - - - - - -

Hum - - - - - - - - - - -

Hum - - - - - - - - - - -

Hum - - - - - - - - - - -

O - jos que cuen - tan es - tre - - - llas,
Eyes that count all of the star - - - light,

pies que se co - rren al mar,
feet that go run to the sea,

amor es la ri - sa en el sue - - ño,
love makes us laugh when we're dream - - - ing,

so - mos de tan - to pen - sar.
we think of so man - y things.

So - mos de tan - to pen - sar.

Hum - - - - - - - - - - - -

¿Quién hizo tantas estrellas?
¿Quién le dio olas al mar?
¿Quién nos dio risa en el sueño?
¿Quién nos dio tanto que pensar?

Who made the stars and so many?
Who gave the waves to the sea?
Who makes us laugh when we're dreaming?
Who makes us think of these things?

Hum melody

Ojos que cuentan estrellas,
pies que se corren al mar,
amor es la risa en el sueño,
somos de tanto pensar.

Eyes that count all of the starlight,
feet that go run to the sea,
love makes us laugh when we're dreaming,
we think of so many things.
Somos de tanto pensar.

48

Las Fronterizas
The Frontier Women

Music and lyrics by Tish Hinojosa

THIS SONG teaches us a little bit of Mexican history about some brave women who fought for the people's rights, alongside the men, during the Mexican Revolution that began in 1910. The song highlights the melodies of two famous songs from that time, "Jesusita en Chihuahua" and "Adelita."

ESTA CANCIÓN nos enseña un poco de las historia mexicana. Se trata de unas mujeres muy valientes que lucharon con los hombres por los derechos de la gente durante la Revolución Mexicana que empezó en 1910. Esta pieza presenta melodías de dos canciones famosas de ese tiempo, "Jesusita en Chihuahua" y "Adelita".

En un tiempo revolucionario
México mil novecientos diez,
se vestían rebeldes norteñas
soldados de cabeza a los pies.

Ritmo de los bailes fronterizos
en sonido de la libertad,
corazones de la tierra amada
se oían en todo lugar.

Once upon a revolutionary
Mexico in nineteen hundred ten,
rebels did whatever necessary,
women fought as soldiers by the men.

While the rhythm of the frontier dances
sounded with the shouts of liberty,
hearts that filled with passion of their country
for the soldier girls they played like this.

Señora Santa Ana

Traditional

THIS SPANISH CRADLE SONG has been sung to babies in Mexico and in South Texas for over a hundred years. I translated it into English so it could be sung to a baby in either language.

ESTA CANCIÓN DE CUNA EN ESPAÑOL ha sido cantada a los bebés en México y en el sur de Texas por más de cien años. La traduje al inglés para que pudiera cantarse en los dos idiomas.

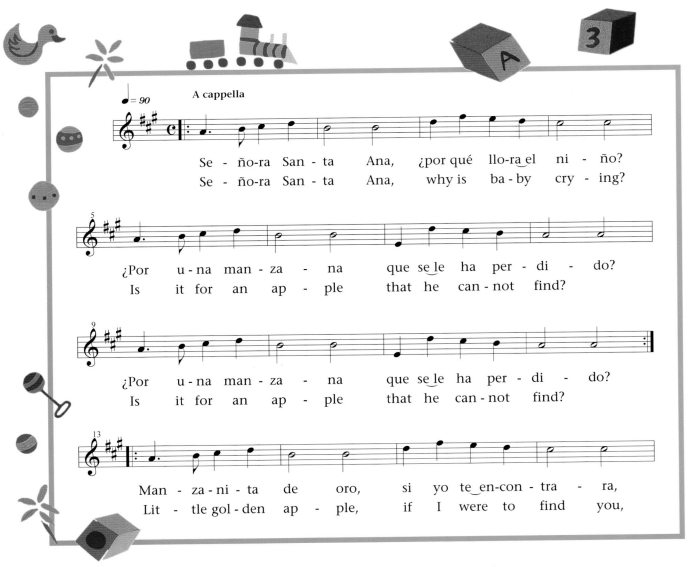

♩ = 90   A cappella

Se - ño-ra San - ta   Ana,   ¿por qué llo-ra_el   ni - ño?
Se - ño-ra San - ta   Ana,   why is   ba - by   cry - ing?

¿Por u - na man - za - na   que se_le ha per - di - do?
Is   it for an ap - ple   that he can - not   find?

¿Por u - na man - za - na   que se_le ha per - di - do?
Is   it for an ap - ple   that he can - not   find?

Man - za - ni - ta de   oro,   si   yo te_en-con - tra - ra,
Lit - tle gol - den ap - ple,   if   I   were to   find   you,

se la die-ra al ni - ño   pa-ra que ca - lla - ra.
I'd give you to my babe   for to calm him, too.

Se la die-ra al ni - ño   pa-ra que ca - lla - ra.
I'd give you to my babe   for to calm him, too.

Duér - me - te, mi ni - ño,   ra - yi - to de sol.
Go to sleep, my ba - by,   lit - tle ray of sun - shine.

Duér - me - te, pe - da - zo   de mi co - ra - zón.
Go to sleep, sweet mor - sel   of this heart of mine.

Fine

Duér - me - te, pe - da - zo   de mi co - ra - zón.
Duér - me - te, pe - da - zo   de mi co - ra - zón.

Señora Santa Ana,
¿por qué llora el niño?
¿Por una manzana
que se le ha perdido?
¿Por una manzana
que se le ha perdido?

Señora Santa Ana,
Why is baby crying?
Is it for an apple
that he cannot find?
Is it for an apple
that he cannot find?

Manzanita de oro,
si yo te encontrara,
se la diera al niño
para que callara.
Se la diera al niño
para que callara.

Little golden apple,
if I were to find you,
I'd give you to my babe
for to calm him, too.
I'd give you to my babe
for to calm him, too.

Duérmete, mi niño,
rayito de sol.
Duérmete, pedazo
de mi corazón.
Duérmete, pedazo
de mi corazón.

Go to sleep, my baby,
little ray of sunshine.
Go to sleep, sweet morsel
of this heart of mine.
Duérmete pedazo
de mi corazón.

Index of Chords

C	Cm	C7	D	Dm
	3fr.			

D7	E	Em	E7	F

Fm		F7	F#	F#m	F#7

G	Gm	G7	A	Am
	3fr.			

A7	B	Bm	B7	G#dim7
				3fr.